The Rite of Baptism for Children

THE RITE OF
BAPTISM
FOR CHILDREN

*The Roman Ritual revised by decree of the Second Vatican
Ecumenical Council by authority of Pope Paul VI*

 **GEOFFREY CHAPMAN**
LONDON DUBLIN MELBOURNE 1970

Geoffrey Chapman Ltd
18 High Street, Wimbledon, London SW 19

Geoffrey Chapman (Ireland) Ltd
5–7 Main Street, Blackrock, County Dublin

First published, this edition, 1970

ISBN 0 225 65816

Translation confirmed by the Sacred Congregation for Divine Worship, 15 April 1970 (Prot. no. 1667/70).

Concordat cum originali: John Humphreys JCD
Secretary to the National Liturgical Commission of England and Wales

Imprimatur: ✠ Victor Guazzelli Westminster: 8.5.70

Printed in the Republic of Ireland by Hely Thom Ltd., Dublin

CONTENTS

GENERAL INTRODUCTION: CHRISTIAN INITIATION

1. Through the sacraments of Christian initiation men and women are freed from the power of darkness. With Christ they die, are buried and rise again. They receive the Spirit of adoption which makes them God's sons and daughters and, with the entire people of God, they celebrate the memorial of the Lord's death and resurrection.[1]

2. Through baptism men and women are incorporated into Christ. They are formed into God's people, and they obtain forgiveness of all their sins. They are raised from their natural human condition to the dignity of adopted children.[2] They become a new creation through water and the Holy Spirit. Hence they are called, and are indeed, the children of God.[3]

Signed with the gift of the Spirit in confirmation, Christians more perfectly become the image of their Lord and are filled with the Holy Spirit. They bear witness to him before all the world and eagerly work for the building up of the body of Christ.[4]

Finally they come to the table of the eucharist, to eat the flesh and drink the blood of the Son of Man so that they may have eternal life[5] and show forth the unity of God's people. By offering themselves with Christ, they share in his universal sacrifice: the entire community of the redeemed is offered to God by their high priest.[6] They pray for a greater outpouring of the Holy Spirit so that the whole human race may be brought into the unity of God's family.[7]

Thus the three sacraments of Christian initiation closely combine to bring the faithful to the full stature of Christ and to enable them to carry out the mission of the entire people of God in the Church and in the world.[8]

I. Dignity of Baptism

3. Baptism is the door to life and to the kingdom of God. Christ offered this first sacrament of the new law to all men that they might have eternal life.[9] He entrusted this sacrament and the gospel to his Church when he told his apostles: 'Go, make disciples of all nations, and baptize them in the name of the Father, and of the Son, and of the Holy Spirit.'[10] Therefore baptism is, above all, the sacrament of that faith by which men and women, enlightened by the Spirit's grace, respond to the gospel of Christ. That is why the Church believes it is her most basic and necessary duty to inspire all, catechumens, parents of children still to be baptized, and godparents, to that true and living faith by which they adhere to Christ and enter into or confirm their commitment to the new covenant. To accomplish this, the Church prescribes the pastoral instruction of catechumens, the preparation of the children's parents, the celebration of God's word, and the profession of baptismal faith.

[1] II Vatican Council, Decree on the Church's Missionary Activity, *Ad Gentes,* 14.
[2] Romans 8:15; Galatians 4:5; Council of Trent, 6th Session, Decree on Justification, Chapter 4, Denz. 796 (1524).
[3] I John 3:1.
[4] II Vatican Council, Decree on the Church's Missionary Activity, *Ad Gentes,* 36.
[5] John 6:55.
[6] Saint Augustine, *The City of God,* X, 6: PL 41, 284; II Vatican Council, Dogmatic Constitution on the Church, *Lumen Gentium,* 11; Decree on the Life and Ministry of Priests, *Presbyterorum Ordinis,* 2.
[7] II Vatican Council, Dogmatic Constitution on the Church, *Lumen Gentium,* 28.
[8] *Ibid.,* 31.
[9] John 3:5.
[10] Matthew 28:19.

4. Further, baptism is the sacrament by which men and women are incorporated into the Church, built into a house where God lives, in the Spirit,[11] into a holy nation and a royal priesthood.[12] It is a sacramental bond of unity linking all who have been signed by it.[13] Because of that unchangeable effect (signified in the Latin liturgy by the anointing of the baptized person with chrism in the presence of God's people), the rite of baptism is held in highest honour by all Christians. It may never lawfully be repeated once it has been validly celebrated, even if by fellow Christians from whom we are separated.

5. Baptism, the cleansing with water by the power of the living Word,[14] makes us sharers in God's own life[15] and his adopted children.[16] As proclaimed in the prayers for the blessing of the water, baptism is a cleansing water of rebirth,[17] which makes us God's children. The blessed Trinity is invoked over those who are to be baptized. Signed in this name, they are consecrated to the Trinity and enter into fellowship with the Father, the Son, and the Holy Spirit. They are prepared for this high dignity and led to it by the scriptural readings, the prayer of the community, and the threefold profession of faith.

6. Far superior to the purifications of the old law, baptism produces all these effects by the power of the mystery of the Lord's passion and resurrection. Those who are baptized are engrafted in the likeness of Christ's death.[18] They are buried with him, they are given life again with him, and with him they rise again.[19] For baptism recalls and effects the paschal mystery itself, because by means of it men and women pass from the death of sin into life. Its celebration, therefore, should reflect the joy of the resurrection, especially when it takes place during the Easter Vigil or on a Sunday.

II. Offices and Ministries of Baptism

7. Christian instruction and the preparation for baptism are a vital concern of God's people, the Church, which hands on and nourishes the faith it has received from the Apostles. Through the ministry of the Church, adults are called by the Holy Spirit to the gospel, and infants are baptized and brought up in this faith. Therefore it is most important that catechists and other lay people should work with priests and deacons in making preparations for baptism. In the actual celebration, the people of God (represented not only by the parents, godparents and relatives, but also, as far as possible, by friends, neighbours, and some members of the local church) should take an active part. Thus they will show their common faith and express their joy as the newly baptized are received into the community of the Church.

8. It is a very ancient custom of the Church that an adult is not admitted to baptism without a godparent, a member of the Christian community who will assist him at least in the final preparation for baptism and after baptism will help him persevere in the faith and in his life as a Christian.

In the baptism of children too, the godparent should be present to be added spiritually to the immediate family of the one to be baptized and to represent Mother Church. As occasion offers, he will be ready to help the parents bring up their child to profess the faith and to show this by living it.

[11] Ephesians 2:22.
[12] 1 Peter 2:9.
[13] II Vatican Council, Decree on Ecumenism, *Unitatis Redintegratio*, 22.
[14] Ephesians 5:26.
[15] 2 Peter 1:4.
[16] Romans 8:15; Galatians 4:5.
[17] Titus 3:5.
[18] Romans 6:4–5.
[19] Ephesians 2:6.

9. At least in the final rites of the catechumenate and in the actual celebration of baptism, the godparent is present to testify to the faith of the adult candidate or, together with the parents, to profess the Church's faith, in which the child is being baptized.

10. Pastors of souls should therefore see to it that the godparent, chosen by the catechumen or by the family, is qualified to carry out his proper liturgical functions as specified in no. 9 above. The godparent should:

    1) be mature enough to undertake this responsibility;

    2) have received the three sacraments of initiation, baptism, confirmation, and the eucharist;

    3) be a member of the Catholic Church, canonically free to carry out this office.

A baptized and believing Christian from a separated church or community may act as a godparent or Christian witness along with a Catholic godparent, at the request of the parents and in accordance with the norms for various ecumenical cases.

11. The ordinary ministers of baptism are bishops, presbyters, and deacons. At every celebration of this sacrament they should remember that they act in the Church in the name of Christ and by the power of the Holy Spirit. They should therefore be diligent in the ministry of the word of God and in the celebration of the sacraments. They must avoid any action which the faithful can rightly condemn as favouritism.[20]

12. Bishops are the principal dispensers of the mysteries of God and leaders of the entire liturgical life in the church committed to them.[21] They thus direct the conferring of baptism, by which a sharing in the kingly priesthood of Christ is granted.[22] Therefore they should personally celebrate baptism, especially at the Easter Vigil. The preparation and baptism of adults is commended to them in a special way.

13. It is the duty of parish priests to assist the bishop in the instruction and baptism of the adults entrusted to his care, unless the bishop makes other provisions. It is also their duty, with the assistance of catechists or other qualified lay people, to prepare the parents and godparents of children with appropriate pastoral guidance and to administer baptism to the children.

14. Other priests and deacons, since they are cooperators in the ministry of bishops and parish priests, also prepare candidates for baptism and, with the invitation or consent of the bishop or parish priest, confer the sacrament.

15. The celebrant may be assisted by other priests and deacons and also by the laity in those parts which pertain to them, especially if there are many persons to be baptized. This provision is made in various parts of the rite.

16. In imminent danger of death and especially at the moment of death, when no priest or deacon is available, any member of the faithful, indeed anyone with the right intention, may and sometimes must administer baptism. If it is a question only of danger of death, then the sacrament should be administered by a member of the faithful if possible, according to the shorter rite (nos. 157–164). Even in this case a small community should be formed to assist at the rite, or at least one or two witnesses should be present if possible.

17. All lay persons, since they belong to the priestly people, and especially parents and, by reason of their work, catechists, obstetricians, women who are employed

[20] II Vatican Council, Constitution on the Sacred Liturgy, *Sacrosanctum Concilium*, 32; Constitution on the Church in the Modern World, *Gaudium et Spes*, 29.

[21] II Vatican Council, Decree on the Bishops' Pastoral Office, *Christus Dominus*, 15.

[22] II Vatican Council, Dogmatic Constitution on the Church, *Lumen Gentium*, 26.

as family or social workers or as nurses of the sick, as well as physicians and surgeons, should know the proper method of baptizing in cases of necessity. They should be taught by parish priests, deacons, and catechists. Bishops should provide appropriate means within their diocese for such instruction.

III. Requirements for the Celebration of Baptism

18. The water used in baptism should be true water, for the sake of the authentic sacramental symbolism. It should be clean, for reasons of health.

19. The baptismal font, or the vessel in which on occasion the water is prepared for the celebration of the sacrament in the sanctuary, should be very clean and attractive.

20. If the climate requires, provision should be made for the water to be heated beforehand.

21. Except in the case of necessity, the priest or deacon should use only water that has been blessed for the rite. The water consecrated at the Easter Vigil should, if possible, be kept and used throughout the Easter season to signify more clearly the relationship between the sacrament of baptism and the paschal mystery. Outside the Easter season, it is desirable that the water be blessed for each occasion, in order that the words of blessing may clearly express the mystery of salvation which the Church recalls and proclaims. If the baptistry is supplied with flowing water, the blessing will be given to the water as it flows.

22. Either the rite of immersion, which is more suitable as a symbol of participation in the death and resurrection of Christ, or the rite of infusion may lawfully be used in the celebration of baptism.

23. The words for baptism in the Latin Church are: 'I baptize you in the name of the Father, and of the Son, and of the Holy Spirit.'

24. A suitable place for celebrating the liturgy of the word of God should be provided in the baptistry or in the church.

25. The baptistry is the area where the baptismal font flows or has been placed. It should be reserved for the sacrament of baptism, and should be a worthy place for Christians to be reborn in water and the Holy Spirit. It may be situated in a chapel either inside or outside the church, or in some other part of the church easily seen by the faithful; it should be large enough to accommodate a good number of people. After the Easter season, the Easter candle should be given a place of honour in the baptistry, so that when it is lighted for the celebration of baptism, the candles of the newly baptized may easily be lighted from it.

26. In the celebration, the parts of the rite which are to be performed outside the baptistry should be celebrated in different areas of the church which most conveniently suit the size of the congregation and the several stages of the baptismal liturgy. When the baptistry cannot accommodate all the catechumens and the congregation, the parts of the rite which are customarily performed in the baptistry may be transferred to some other suitable area of the church.

27. As far as possible, all recently born babies should be baptized at a common celebration on the same day. Except for a good reason, baptism should not be celebrated more than once on the same day in the same church.

28. Further details concerning the time of baptism of adults and children will be found in the respective rites. The celebration of the sacrament should always suggest its paschal character.

29. Parish priests should carefully and without delay record in the baptismal register the names of those baptized, the minister, parents and godparents, and the place and date of baptisim.

IV. Adaptations by Conferences of Bishops

30. According to the Constitution on the Sacred Liturgy (no. 63b), it is within the competence of conferences of bishops to compose for their local rituals a section corresponding to this one in the Roman Ritual, adapted to the needs of their respective regions. When this has been reviewed by the Apostolic See, it should be used in the regions for which it was prepared.

In this connection, it is the responsibility of the conferences of bishops:

1) to determine the adaptations, according to no. 39 of the Constitution on the Sacred Liturgy;

2) carefully and prudently to consider what elements of a country's distinctive culture may suitably be admitted into divine worship. Adaptations considered useful or necessary should then be submitted to the Apostolic See, with whose consent they may be introduced.

3) to retain distinctive elements of existing local rituals as long as they conform with the Constitution on the Sacred Liturgy and correspond to contemporary needs; or to modify these elements;

4) to prepare translations of the texts that genuinely reflect the characteristics of various languages and cultures and to add music for the texts when appropriate;

5) to adapt and augment the introduction contained in the Roman Ritual, so that the ministers may fully understand the meaning of the rites and express this effectively in action;

6) to arrange the material in the various editions of the liturgical books prepared under the guidance of the conferences of bishops so that these books may be best suited for pastoral use.

31. As stated in nos. 37-40 and 65 of the Constitution on the Sacred Liturgy, it is the responsibility of the conferences of bishops in mission countries to judge whether certain initiation ceremonies in use among some peoples can be adapted for the rite of Christian baptism and to decide whether these rites are to be incorporated into it.

32. When the Roman Ritual for baptism provides a choice of several formulas, local rituals may add other formulas of the same kind.

33. The celebration of baptism is greatly enhanced by the use of song. It stimulates a sense of unity among those present, it gives warmth to their common prayer, and it expresses the joy of Easter. Conferences of bishops should encourage and help musical specialists to compose settings for texts suitable for congregational singing at baptism.

V. Adaptations by the Minister of Baptism

34. The minister, taking into account existing circumstances and needs, as well as the wishes of the faithful, should freely use the various choices allowed in the rite.

35. In addition to the adaptations which are provided in the Roman Ritual for the dialogue and blessings, the minister may make other adaptations for special circumstances. These adaptations will be indicated more fully in the introduction to the rites of baptism for adults and for children.

BAPTISM OF CHILDREN

Introduction

I. Importance of Baptizing Children

1. Children or infants are those who have not yet reached the age of discernment and therefore cannot have or profess personal faith.

2. From the earliest times, the Church, to which the mission of preaching the gospel and of baptizing was entrusted, has baptized children as well as adults. Our Lord said: 'Unless a man is reborn in water and the Holy Spirit, he cannot enter the kingdom of God.'[1] The Church has always understood these words to mean that children should not be deprived of baptism, because they are baptized in the faith of the Church. This faith is proclaimed for them by their parents and godparents, who represent both the local Church and the whole society of saints and believers: 'The Church is at once the mother of all and the mother of each.'[2]

3. To fulfill the true meaning of the sacrament, children must later be formed in the faith in which they have been baptized. The foundation of this formation will be the sacrament itself, which they have already received. Christian formation, which is their due, seeks to lead them gradually to learn God's plan in Christ, so that they may ultimately accept for themselves the faith in which they have been baptized.

II. Ministries and Roles in the Celebration of Baptism

4. The people of God, that is the Church, made present in the local community, has an important part to play in the baptism of both children and adults.

Before and after the celebration of the sacrament, the child has a right to the love and help of the community. During the rite, in addition to the ways of congregational participation mentioned in no. 7 of the general introduction, the community exercises its duty when it expresses its assent together with the celebrant after the profession of faith by the parents and godparents. In this way it is clear that the faith in which the children are baptized is not the private possession of the individual family, but is the common treasure of the whole Church of Christ.

5. Because of the natural relationships, parents have a more important ministry and role in the baptism of infants than the godparents.

1) Before the celebration of the sacrament, it is of great importance that parents, moved by their own faith or with the help of friends or other members of the community, should prepare to take part in the rite with understanding. They should be provided with suitable means such as books, instructions, and catechisms written for families. The parish priest should make it his duty to visit them, or see that they are visited, as a family or as a group of families, and prepare them for the coming celebration by pastoral counsel and common prayer.

2) It is very important that the parents should be present in the celebration in which their child is reborn in water and the Holy Spirit.

3) In the celebration of baptism, the father and mother have special parts to play. They listen to the words addressed to them by the celebrant, they join in prayer along with the congregation, and they exercise a special function when: a) they publicly ask that the child be baptized; b) they sign their child with the sign of the cross after the celebrant; c) they renounce Satan and make their profession of faith; d) they (and especially the mother) carry the child to the font; e) they hold the

---

[1] John 3:5.
[2] Saint Augustine, Epistle 98, 5: PL 33, 362.

lighted candle; f) they are blessed with the special prayers for the mothers and fathers.

4) If one of the parents cannot make the profession of faith (if, for example, he is not a Catholic), he may keep silent. All that is asked of him, when he requests baptism for the child, is that he should make arrangements, or at least give permission, for the child to be instructed in the faith of its baptism.

5) After baptism it is the responsibility of the parents, in their gratitude to God and in fidelity to the duty they have undertaken, to enable the child to know God, whose adopted child it has become, to receive confirmation, and to participate in the holy eucharist. In this duty they are again to be helped by the parish priest by suitable means.

6. Each child may have a godfather and a godmother; the word 'godparents' is used in the rite to describe both.

7. In addition to what is said about the ordinary minister of baptism in the general introduction (nos. 11–15), the following should be noted:

1) It is the duty of the priest to prepare families for the baptism of their children and to help them in the task of Christian formation which they have undertaken. It is the duty of the bishop to coordinate such pastoral efforts in the diocese, with the help also of deacons and lay people.

2) It is also the duty of the priest to arrange that baptism is always celebrated with proper dignity and, as far as possible, adapted to the circumstances and wishes of the families concerned. Everyone who performs the rite of baptism should do so with care and devotion; he must also try to be understanding and friendly to all.

III. Time and Place for the Baptism of Children

8. As for the time of baptism, the first consideration is the welfare of the child, that it may not be deprived of the benefit of the sacrament; then the health of the mother must be considered, so that, as far as possible she too may be present. Then, as long as they do not interfere with the greater good of the child, there are pastoral considerations such as allowing sufficient time to prepare the parents and for planning the actual celebration to bring out its paschal character:

1) If the child is in danger of death, it is to be baptized without delay, as is laid down in no. 21.

2) In other cases, as soon as possible and even before the child is born, the parents should be in touch with the parish priest concerning the baptism, so that proper preparation may be made for the celebration.

3) An infant should be baptized within the first weeks after birth. The conference of bishops may, for sufficiently serious pastoral reasons, determine a longer interval of time between birth and baptism.

4) When the parents are not yet prepared to profess the faith or to undertake the duty of bringing up their children as Christians, it is for the parish priest, keeping in mind whatever regulations may have been laid down by the conference of bishops, to determine the time for the baptism of infants.

9. To bring out the paschal character of baptism, it is recommended that the sacrament be celebrated during the Easter Vigil or on Sunday, when the Church commemorates the Lord's resurrection. On Sunday, baptism may be celebrated even during Mass, so that the entire community may be present and the necessary relationship between baptism and eucharist may be clearly seen, but this should not be done too often. Regulations for the celebration of baptism during the Easter Vigil or at Mass on Sunday are set out below.

10. So that baptism may clearly appear as the sacrament of the Church's faith and of admittance into the people of God, it should normally be celebrated in the parish church, which must have a baptismal font.

11. The bishop, after consulting the local parish priest, may permit or direct that a baptismal font be placed in another church or public oratory within the parish boundaries. In these places, too, it is the normal right of the parish priest to celebrate baptism.

12. Except in case of danger of death, baptism should not be celebrated in private houses.

13. Unless the bishop decides otherwise (see no. 11), baptism should not be celebrated in hospitals, except in cases of emergency or for some other pastoral reason of a pressing kind. Care should always be taken that the parish priest is notified and that the parents are suitably prepared beforehand.

14. While the liturgy of the word is being celebrated, it is desirable that the children should be taken to some other place. Provision should be made for the mothers or godmothers to attend the liturgy of the word; the children should therefore be entrusted to the care of other women.

IV. Structure of the Rite of Baptizing Children

A. Order of Baptism Celebrated by the Ordinary Minister

15. Baptism, whether for one child, or for several, or even for a larger number, should be celebrated by the ordinary minister and with the full rite when there is no immediate danger of death.

16. The rite begins with the reception of the children. This is to indicate the desire of the parents and godparents, as well as the intention of the Church, concerning the celebration of the sacrament of baptism. These purposes are expressed in action when the parents and the celebrant trace the sign of the cross on the foreheads of the children.

17. Then the liturgy of the word is directed toward stirring up the faith of the parents, godparents, and congregation, and praying in common for the fruits of baptism before the sacrament itself. This part of the celebration consists of the reading of one or more passages from holy scripture; a homily, followed by a period of silence; the prayer of the faithful; and finally a prayer, drawn up in the style of an exorcism, to introduce either the anointing with the oil of catechumens or the laying on of hands.

18. 1) The celebration of the sacrament is immediately preceded by:
   a) the solemn prayer of the celebrant, who, by invoking God and recalling his plan of salvation, blesses the water of baptism or commemorates its previous blessing;
   b) the renunciation of Satan on the part of parents and godparents, and their profession of faith, to which is added the assent of the celebrant and the community; and the final interrogation of the parents and godparents.
   2) The celebration of the sacrament is performed by washing in water, by way of immersion or infusion, according to local custom, and by the invocation of the blessed Trinity.
   3) The celebration of the sacrament is completed, first by the anointing with chrism, which signifies the royal priesthood of the baptized and enrolment in

the fellowship of God's people; then by the ceremonies of the white garment, lighted candle, and *Ephphetha* (the last of which is optional).

19. After the celebrant speaks of the future reception of the eucharist by the baptized children, the Lord's Prayer, in which God's children pray to their Father in heaven, is recited before the altar. Finally, a prayer of blessing is said over the mothers, fathers, and all present, to ask God's grace in abundance for all.

B. Shorter Rite of Baptism

20. In the shorter rite of baptism designed for the use of catechists,[3] the reception of the children, the celebration of the word of God, or the instruction by the minister, and the prayer of the faithful are retained. Before the font, the minister offers a prayer invoking God and recalling the history of salvation as it relates to baptism. After the baptismal washing, an adapted formula is recited in place of the anointing with chrism, and the whole rite concludes in the customary way. The omissions, therefore, are the exorcism, the anointing with oil of catechumens and with chrism, and the *Ephphetha*.

21. The shorter rite for baptizing a child in danger of death and in the absence of the ordinary minister has a twofold structure:
   1) At the moment of death or when there is urgency because of imminent danger of death, the minister,[4] omitting all other ceremonies, pours water (not necessarily blessed but real and natural water), on the head of the child, and pronounces the customary formula.[5]
   2) If it is prudently judged that there is sufficient time, several of the faithful may be gathered together, and, if one of them is able to lead the others in a short prayer, the following rite may be used:

   an explanation by the minister of the sacrament, a short common prayer, the profession of faith by the parents or one godparent, and the pouring of the water with the customary words. But if those present are uneducated, the minister of the sacrament should recite the profession of faith aloud and baptize according to the rite for use at the moment of death.

22. In danger of death, the priest or deacon may also use this shorter form if necessary. If there is time and he has the sacred chrism, the parish priest or other priest enjoying the same faculty should not fail to confer confirmation after baptism. In this case he omits the postbaptismal anointing with chrism.

V. Adaptations by Conferences of Bishops or by Bishops

23. In addition to the adaptations provided for in the general introduction (nos. 30–33), the baptismal rite for infants admits other variations, to be determined by the conferences of bishops.

24. As is indicated in the Roman Ritual, the following matters are left to the discretion of the conferences:
   1) As local customs may dictate, the questioning about the name of the child may be arranged in different ways: the name may have been given already or may be given during the rite of baptism.
   2) The anointing with oil of catechumens may be omitted (nos. 50, 87).
   3) The formula of renunciation may be shortened or extended (nos. 57, 94, 121).

---

[3] II Vatican Council, Constitution on the Sacred Liturgy, *Sacrosanctum Concilium,* 68.
[4] General Introduction, 16.
[5] *Ibid.,* 23.

    4) If the number to be baptized is very great, the anointing with chrism may be omitted (no. 125).

    5) The rite of *Ephphetha* may be retained (nos. 65, 101).

25. In many countries parents are sometimes not ready for the celebration of baptism or they ask for their children to be baptized, although the latter will not afterwards receive a Christian education and will even lose the faith. Since it is not enough to instruct the parents and to inquire about their faith in the course of the rite itself, conferences of bishops may issue pastoral directives, for the guidance of parish priests, to determine a longer interval between birth and baptism.

26. It is for the bishop to judge whether in his diocese catechists may give an improvised homily or speak only from a written text.

VI. Adaptations by the Minister

27. During meetings to prepare the parents for the baptism of their children, it is important that the instruction should be supported by prayer and religious rites. The various elements provided in the rite of baptism for the celebration of the word of God will prove helpful.

28. When the baptism of children is celebrated as part of the Easter Vigil, the ritual should be arranged as follows:

    1) At a convenient time and place before the Easter Vigil, the rite of receiving the children is celebrated. The liturgy of the word may be omitted at the end, according to circumstances, and the prayer of exorcism is said, followed by the anointing with oil of catechumens.

    2) The celebration of the sacrament (nos. 56–58, 60–63) takes place after the blessing of the water, as is indicated in the Rite of the Easter Vigil.

    3) The assent of the celebrant and community (no. 59) is omitted, as are the presentation of the lighted candle (no. 64) and the rite of *Ephphetha* (no. 65).

    4) The conclusion of the rite (nos. 67–71) is omitted.

29. If baptism takes place during Sunday Mass, the Mass for that Sunday is used, and the celebration takes place as follows:

    1) The rite of receiving the children (nos. 33–43) takes place at the beginning of Mass, and the greeting and penitential rite are omitted.

    2) In the liturgy of the word:

    a) The readings are taken from the Mass of the Sunday or, for special reasons, from those provided in the baptismal rite.

    b) The homily is based on the sacred texts, but should take account of the baptism which is to take place.

    c) The creed is not said, since the profession of faith by the entire community before baptism takes its place.

    d) The general intercessions are taken from those used in the rite of baptism (nos. 47–48, 217–220). At the end, however, before the invocation of the saints, petitions are added for the universal Church and the needs of the world.

    3) The celebration of baptism continues with the prayer of exorcism, anointing, and other ceremonies in the rite (nos. 49–66).

    4) After the celebration of baptism, the Mass continues in the usual way with the offertory.

    5) For the blessing at the end of Mass, the priest may use one of the formulas provided in the rite of baptism (nos. 70, 247–249).

30. If baptism is celebrated during Mass on weekdays, it is arranged in the same way as on Sundays; the readings for the liturgy of the word may be taken from those that are provided in the rite of baptism (nos. 44, 186–194, 204–215).

31. In accordance with no. 34 of the general introduction, the minister may make some adaptations in the rite, as circumstances require, such as:

1) If the child's mother died in childbirth, this should be taken into account in the opening instruction (no. 36), general intercessions (nos. 47, 217–220), and final blessing (nos. 70, 247–248).

2) In the dialogue with the parents (nos. 37–38, 76–77), their answers should be taken into account: if they have not answered 'baptism,' but 'faith,' or 'the grace of Christ,' or 'entrance into the Church,' or 'everlasting life,' then the minister does not begin by saying 'baptism,' but uses 'faith,' or 'the grace of Christ,' and so forth.

3) The rite of bringing a baptized child to the church (nos. 165–185), which has been drawn up for use only when the child has been baptized in danger of death, should be adapted to cover other contingencies, for example, when children have been baptized during a time of religious persecution or temporary disagreement between the parents.

In England and Wales, the Hierarchy direct that the anointing with the oil of catechumens is not to be omitted; the Ephphetha need not be performed unless specially requested by the parents, and then only after explanation to the people; baptism is to be conferred on children as soon as possible after the mother has recovered from childbirth, and should not be delayed for more than one month after the birth of the child, except for serious reasons. (See paras. 24 and 25.)

In Ireland, the Hierarchy direct that the anointing with the oil of catechumens and the Ephphetha are to be retained (see para. 24). The alternative text of the Our Father is permitted.

In Scotland, the Hierarchy direct that the anointing with the oil of catechumens and the Ephphetha are to be retained (see para. 24).

RITE OF BAPTISM FOR SEVERAL CHILDREN

Reception of the Children

32. If possible, baptism should take place on Sunday, the day on which the Church celebrates the paschal mystery. It should be conferred in a communal celebration for all the recently born children, and in the presence of the faithful, or at least of relatives, friends, and neighbours, who are all to take an active part in the rite.

33. It is the role of the father and mother, accompanied by the godparents, to present the child to the Church for baptism.

34. If there are very many children, and if there are several priests or deacons present, these may help the celebrant in the parts referred to below.

35. The people may sing a psalm or hymn suitable for the occasion. Meanwhile the celebrating priest or deacon, vested in alb or surplice, with a stole (with or without a cope) of festive colour, and accompanied by the ministers, goes to the entrance of the church or to that part of the church where the parents and godparents are waiting with those who are to be baptized.

36. The celebrant greets all present, and especially the parents and godparents, reminding them briefly of the joy with which the parents welcomed their children as gifts from God, the source of life, who now wishes to bestow his own life on these little ones.

37. First the celebrant questions the parents of each child.

Celebrant. **What name do you give your child ?** (or: **have you given ?**)

Parents. **N.**

Celebrant. **What do you ask of God's Church for N. ?**

Parents. **Baptism.**

The celebrant may choose other words for this dialogue.

The first reply may be given by someone other than the parents if local custom gives him the right to name the child.

In the second response the parents may use other words, e.g., 'faith,' 'the grace of Christ,' 'entrance into the Church,' 'eternal life.'

---

38. If there are many children to be baptized, the celebrant asks the names from all the parents together, and each family replies in turn. If there is a very large number of children, this question may be omitted altogether. The second question may also be asked of all together.

Celebrant. **What name do you give each of these children ?** (or: **have you given ?**)

Parents. **N., N., etc.**

Celebrant. **What do you ask of God's Church for your children ?**

All. **Baptism.**

---

39. The celebrant speaks to the parents in these or similar words:

Celebrant. **You have asked to have your children baptized. In doing so you are accepting the responsibility of training them in the practice of the faith. It will be your duty to bring them up to keep God's commandments as Christ taught us, by loving God and our neighbour. Do you clearly understand what you are undertaking ?**

Parents. **We do.**

This response is given by each family individually. But if there are many children to be baptized, the response may be given by all together.

40. Then the celebrant turns to the godparents and addresses them in these or similar words:

Celebrant. **Are you ready to help these parents in their duty as Christian mothers and fathers?**

All the Godparents. **We are.**

41. *Celebrant.* **N. and N. (or My dear children), the Christian community welcomes you with great joy. In its name I claim you for Christ our Saviour by the sign of his cross. I now trace the cross on your foreheads, and invite your parents (and godparents) to do the same.**

He signs each child on the forehead, in silence. Then he invites the parents and (if it seems appropriate) the godparents to do the same.

---

[111] If there is a very large number of children, the celebrant says instead:

Celebrant. **My dear children, the Christian community welcomes you with great joy. In its name I claim you for Christ our Saviour by the sign of his cross.**

He makes the sign of the cross over all the children together, and says:

Celebrant. **Parents (or godparents), make the sign of Christ our Saviour on the foreheads of your children.**

Then the parents (or godparents) sign the children on their foreheads.

---

42. The celebrant invites the parents, godparents, and the others to take part in the liturgy of the word. If circumstances permit, there is a procession to the place where this will be celebrated, during which a song is sung, e.g., Psalm 84:7, 8, 9ab.

43. The children to be baptized may be carried to a separate place, where they remain until the end of the liturgy of the word.

Celebration of God's Word

Scriptural Readings and Homily

44. One or even two of the following gospel passages are read, during which all may sit if convenient.

A reading from the holy Gospel according to John.

Unless a man is born again, he cannot see the kingdom of heaven. (3:1–6)

There was one of the Pharisees called Nicodemus, a leading Jew, who came to Jesus by night and said, 'Rabbi, we know that you are a teacher who comes from God; for no one could perform the signs that you do unless God were with him'. Jesus answered:
> **'I tell you most solemnly,**
> **unless a man is born from above,**
> **he cannot see the kingdom of God.'**

Nicodemus said, 'How can a grown man be born? Can he go back into his mother's womb and be born again?' Jesus replied:
> **'I tell you most solemnly,**
> **unless a man is born through water and the Spirit,**
> **he cannot enter the kingdom of God:**
> **what is born of the flesh is flesh;**
> **what is born of the Spirit is spirit.'**

This is the Gospel of the Lord.

A reading from the holy Gospel according to Matthew.

Make disciples of all the nations; baptize them in the name of the
Father and of the Son and of the Holy Spirit. (28:18–20)

Jesus came up and spoke to his disciples. He said, 'All authority in heaven and
on earth has been given to me. Go, therefore, make disciples of all the nations;
baptize them in the name of the Father and of the Son and of the Holy Spirit,
and teach them to observe all the commands I gave you. And know that I am
with you always; yes, to the end of time.'

This is the Gospel of the Lord.

A reading from the holy Gospel according to Mark.

He was baptized in the Jordan by John. (1:9–11)

Jesus came from Nazareth in Galilee and was baptized in the Jordan by John.
No sooner had he come up out of the water than he saw the heavens torn apart
and the Spirit, like a dove, descending on him. And a voice came from heaven,
'You are my Son, the Beloved; my favour rests on you'.

This is the Gospel of the Lord.

A reading from the holy Gospel according to Mark.

Let the little children come to me. (10:13–16)

People were bringing little children to Jesus, for him to touch them. The disciples
turned them away, but when Jesus saw this he was indignant and said to them, 'Let
the little children come to me; do not stop them; for it is to such as these that the
kingdom of God belongs. I tell you solemnly, anyone who does not welcome the
kingdom of God like a little child will never enter it.' Then he put his arms round them,
laid his hands on them and gave them his blessing.

This is the Gospel of the Lord.

The passages given in the *Lectionary* (at Baptism of Infants, pp. 882–887) may be chosen, or other passages which
better meet the wishes or needs of the parents. Between the readings, responsorial psalms or verses may be sung as
given in the *Lectionary*.

45. After the reading, the celebrant gives a short homily, explaining to those present the significance of what has been
read. His purpose will be to lead them to a deeper understanding of the mystery of baptism and to encourage the
parents and godparents to a ready acceptance of the responsibilities which arise from the sacrament.

46. After the homily, or in the course of or after the litany, it is desirable to have a period of silence while all pray at
the invitation of the celebrant. If convenient, a suitable song follows, e.g., one chosen from nos. 224–244.

Intercessions (Prayer of the Faithful)

47. *Celebrant.* **My brothers and sisters,* let us ask our Lord Jesus Christ to look
lovingly on these children who are to be baptized, on their parents and godparents,
and on all the baptized.**

---

*At the discretion of the priest, other words which seem more suitable under the circumstances, such as my dear
people, friends, dearly beloved, brethren, may be used. This also applies to parallel instances in the liturgy.

Leader. By the mystery of your death and resurrection, bathe these children in light, give them the new life of baptism and welcome them into your holy Church.*

All. Lord, hear our prayer.

Leader. Through baptism and confirmation, make them your faithful followers and witnesses to your gospel.

All. Lord, hear our prayer.

Leader. Lead them by a holy life to the joys of God's kingdom.

All. Lord, hear our prayer.

Leader. Make the lives of their parents and godparents examples of faith to inspire these children.

All. Lord, hear our prayer.

Leader. Keep their families always in your love.

All. Lord, hear our prayer.

Leader. Renew the grace of our baptism in each one of us.

All. Lord, hear our prayer.

Other forms may be chosen from nos. 217–220, see below, pp. 46–48.

48. The celebrant next invites all present to invoke the saints. At this point, if the children have been taken out, they are brought back. Where there is a very large number of children, the invocation of the saints may be omitted.

Holy Mary, Mother of God	pray for us
Saint Joseph	pray for us
Saint John the Baptist	pray for us
Saint Peter and Saint Paul	pray for us

The names of other saints may be added, especially the patrons of the children to be baptized, and of the church or locality. The litany concludes:

All you saints of God	pray for us

Prayer of Exorcism and Anointing before Baptism

When no priest or deacon is present, this is omitted.

49. *Celebrant.* Almighty and ever-living God,
you sent your only Son into the world
to cast out the power of Satan, spirit of evil,
to rescue man from the kingdom of darkness,
and bring him into the splendour of your kingdom of light.
We pray for these children:
set them free from original sin,
make them temples of your glory,
and send your Holy Spirit to dwell within them.
(We ask this) through Christ our Lord.   *All.* Amen.

* In England, Wales and Scotland, petitions of the Prayer of the Faithful here, and in parallel instances, end with the usual formula, thus: *Leader:* Lord, hear us. *All:* Lord, graciously hear us.

Another form of the prayer of exorcism:

[221]

Celebrant. Almighty God,
you sent your only Son
to rescue us from the slavery of sin,
and to give us the freedom
only your sons and daughters enjoy.

We now pray for these children
who will have to face the world with its temptations,
and fight the devil in all his cunning.

Your Son died and rose again to save us.
By his victory over sin and death,
bring these children out of the power of darkness.
Strengthen them with the grace of Christ,
and watch over them at every step in life's journey.
(We ask this) through Christ our Lord.   *All.* Amen.

50. *Celebrant.* We anoint you with the oil of salvation
in the name of Christ our Saviour;
may he strengthen you
with his power,
who lives and reigns for ever and ever.   *All.* Amen.

He anoints each child on the breast with the oil of catechumens. If the number of children is large, the anointing may be done by several ministers.

51. If, for serious reasons, the conference of bishops so decides, the anointing before baptism may be omitted. In that case the celebrant says once only:

Celebrant. **May you have strength in the power of Christ our Saviour, who lives and reigns for ever and ever.**   *All.* Amen.

And immediately he lays his hand on each child in silence.

Where there is a very large number of children to be baptized, the celebrant does not anoint them with the oil of catechumens. He imposes his hands over all the children at once and says:

Celebrant. **May you have strength in the power of Christ our Saviour, who lives and reigns for ever and ever.**   *All. Amen*.

52. If the baptistry is located outside the church or is not within view of the congregation, all go there in procession. If the baptistry is located within view of the congregation, the celebrant, parents, and godparents go there with the children, while the others remain in their places.

If, however, the baptistry cannot accommodate the congregation, the baptism may be celebrated in a suitable place within the church, and the parents and godparents bring the child forward at the proper moment.

Meanwhile, if it can be done suitably, an appropriate song is sung, e.g., Psalm 22.

Celebration of the Sacrament

53. When they come to the font, the celebrant briefly reminds the congregation of the wonderful work of God whose plan it is to sanctify man, body and soul, through water. He may use these or similar words:

Celebrant. **My dear brothers and sisters, we now ask God to give these children new life in abundance through water and the Holy Spirit.**

or:

Celebrant. My dear brothers and sisters, God uses the sacrament of water to give his divine life to those who believe in him. Let us turn to him, and ask him to pour his gift of life from this font on the children he has chosen.

Blessing and Invocation of God over Baptismal Water (outside the Easter season)

When no priest is present, the form of Blessing and Invocation of God over Baptismal Water is that set out below, pp. 51–52, nos. 141–143.

54. Then turning to the font, he says the following blessing:

Celebrant. Father, you give us grace through sacramental signs, which tell us of the wonders of your unseen power.
In baptism we use your gift of water, which you have made a rich symbol of the grace you give us in this sacrament.
At the very dawn of creation your Spirit breathed on the waters, making them the wellspring of all holiness.
The waters of the great flood you made a sign of the waters of baptism, that make an end of sin and a new beginning of goodness.
Through the waters of the Red Sea you led Israel out of slavery, to be an image of God's holy people, set free from sin by baptism.
In the waters of the Jordan your Son was baptized by John and anointed with the Spirit.
Your Son willed that water and blood should flow from his side as he hung upon the cross.
After his resurrection he told his disciples: 'Go out and teach all nations, baptizing them in the name of the Father, and of the Son, and of the Holy Spirit.'
Father, look now with love upon your Church, and unseal for her the fountain of baptism.
By the power of the Spirit give to the water of this font the grace of your Son.
You created man in your own likeness: cleanse him from sin in a new birth to innocence by water and the Spirit.

The celebrant touches the water with his right hand and continues:

We ask you, Father, with your Son to send the Holy Spirit upon the water of this font. May all who are buried with Christ in the death of baptism rise also with him to newness of life. (We ask this) through Christ our Lord.   *All.* Amen.

Other forms of the blessing:

1. *Celebrant.* Praise to you, almighty God and Father, for you have created   [223]
water to cleanse and to give life.

All. Blessed be God (or some other suitable acclamation by the people).

Celebrant. Praise to you, Lord Jesus Christ, the Father's only Son, for you offered yourself on the cross, that in the blood and water flowing from your side, and through your death and resurrection, the Church might be born.

All. Blessed be God.

Celebrant. Praise to you, God the Holy Spirit, for you anointed Christ at his baptism in the waters of Jordan, so that we might all be baptized into you.

All. Blessed be God.

Celebrant. Come to us, Lord, Father of all, and make holy this water which you have created, so that all who are baptized in it may be washed clean of sin, and be born again to live as your children.

All. Hear us, Lord (or some other suitable invocation).

Celebrant. Make this water holy, Lord, so that all who are baptized into Christ's death and resurrection by this water may become more perfectly like your Son.

All. Hear us, Lord.

The celebrant touches the water with his right hand and continues:

Celebrant. Lord, make holy this water which you have created, so that all those whom you have chosen may be born again by the power of the Holy Spirit, and may take their place among your holy people.

All. Hear us, Lord.

If the baptismal water has already been blessed, the celebrant omits the invocation *Come to us, Lord* and those which follow it, and says:

Celebrant. You have called your children, N., N., to this cleansing water that they may share in the faith of your Church and have eternal life. By the mystery of this consecrated water lead them to a new and spiritual birth. (We ask this) through Christ our Lord.   *All.* Amen

2. *Celebrant.* Father, God of mercy, through these waters of baptism you [224] have filled us with new life as your very own children.

All. Blessed be God (or some other suitable acclamation by the people).

Celebrant. From all who are baptized in water and the Holy Spirit, you have formed one people, united in your Son Jesus Christ.

All. Blessed be God.

Celebrant. You have set us free and filled our hearts with the Spirit of your love, that we may live in your peace.

All. Blessed be God.

Celebrant. You call those who have been baptized to announce the Good News of Jesus Christ to people everywhere.

All. Blessed be God.

Celebrant. You have called your children, N., N., to this cleansing water and new birth that by sharing the faith of your Church they might have eternal life. Bless ✠ this water in which they will be baptized. We ask this in the name of Christ our Lord.   *All.* Amen.

If the baptismal water has already been blessed, the celebrant omits this last prayer and says:

Celebrant. You have called your children, N., N., to this cleansing water that they may share in the faith of your Church and have eternal life. By the mystery of this consecrated water lead them to a new and spiritual birth. (We ask this) through Christ our Lord. *All.* **Amen.**

---

55. During the Easter season, if there is baptismal water which was consecrated at the Easter Vigil, the blessing and invocation of God over the water are nevertheless included, so that this theme of thanksgiving and petition may find a place in the baptism. The forms of this blessing and invocation are those given above as alternatives 1, 2 [nos. 223, 224], with the variation indicated at the end of each text.

Renunciation of Sin and Profession of Faith

56. The celebrant speaks to the parents and godparents in these words:

Celebrant. **Dear parents and godparents:**
You have come here to present these children for baptism. By water and the Holy Spirit they are to receive the gift of new life from God, who is love.
On your part, you must make it your constant care to bring them up in the practice of the faith. See that the divine life which God gives them is kept safe from the poison of sin, to grow always stronger in their hearts.
If your faith makes you ready to accept this responsibility, renew now the vows of your own baptism. Reject sin; profess your faith in Christ Jesus. This is the faith of the Church. This is the faith in which these children are about to be baptized.

57. The celebrant questions the parents and godparents.

Celebrant. **Do you reject Satan?**
Parents and godparents. **I do.**

Celebrant. **And all his works?**
Parents and godparents. **I do.**

Celebrant. **And all his empty promises?**
Parents and godparents. **I do.**

Alternative form of questioning.

Celebrant. **Do you reject sin, so as to live in the freedom of God's children?**
Parents and godparents. **I do.**

Celebrant. **Do you reject the glamour of evil, and refuse to be mastered by sin?**
Parents and godparents. **I do.**

Celebrant. **Do you reject Satan, father of sin and prince of darkness?**
Parents and godparents. **I do.**

According to circumstances, this second form may be expressed with greater precision by the conferences of bishops, especially in places where it is necessary for the parents and godparents to reject superstitious and magical practices used with children.

58. Next the celebrant asks for the threefold profession of faith from the parents and godparents:

Celebrant. **Do you believe in God, the Father almighty, creator of heaven and earth?**

Parents and godparents. **I do.**

Celebrant. **Do you believe in Jesus Christ, his only Son, our Lord, who was born of the Virgin Mary, was crucified, died, and was buried, rose from the dead, and is now seated at the right hand of the Father?**

Parents and godparents. **I do.**

Celebrant. **Do you believe in the Holy Spirit, the holy catholic Church, the communion of saints, the forgiveness of sins, the resurrection of the body, and life everlasting?**

Parents and godparents. **I do.**

59. The celebrant and the congregation give their assent to this profession of faith:

Celebrant. **This is our faith. This is the faith of the Church. We are proud to profess it, in Christ Jesus our Lord.**   *All.* **Amen.**

If desired, some other formula may be used instead, or a suitable song by which the community expresses its faith with a single voice.

Baptism

60. The celebrant invites the first of the families to the font. Using the name of the individual child, he questions the parents and godparents.

---

[124] Where there is a very large number of children to be baptized, and if there are several ministers, each of them questions the parents and godparents, using the name of the individual child.

Celebrant. **Is it your will that** N. **should be baptized in the faith of the Church, which we have all professed with you?**

Parents and godparents. **It is.**

He baptizes the child, saying:

Celebrant. N., **I baptize you in the name of the Father,**

He immerses the child or pours water upon it.

and of the Son,

He immerses the child or pours water upon it a second time.

and of the Holy Spirit.

He immerses the child or pours water upon it a third time.
He asks the same question and performs the same action for each child.
After each baptism it is appropriate for the people to sing a short acclamation. (See nos. 225–245, pp. 49–50.)

If the baptism is performed by the pouring of water, it is preferable that the child be held by the mother (or father). Where, however, it is felt that the existing custom should be retained, the godmother (or godfather) may hold the child. If baptism is by immersion, the mother or father (godmother or godfather) lifts the child out of the font.

61. If the number of children to be baptized is large, and other priests or deacons are present, these may baptize some of the children in the way described above, and with the same form.

Anointing with Chrism

62. *Celebrant.* **God the Father of our Lord Jesus Christ has freed you from sin, given you a new birth by water and the Holy Spirit, and welcomed you into his holy people. He now anoints you with the chrism of salvation. As Christ was anointed Priest, Prophet, and King, so may you live always as members of his body, sharing everlasting life.** *All.* **Amen.**

Next, the celebrant anoints each child on the crown of the head with chrism, in silence.
If the number of children is large and other priests or deacons are present, these may anoint some of the children with chrism.

If the number of children is extremely large, the conference of bishops may decide that the anointing with chrism may be omitted. It is omitted when no priest is present. In this case, an adapted formula is used:

Celebrant. **God the Father of our Lord Jesus Christ has freed you from sin, and has given you a new birth by water and the Holy Spirit. He has made you Christians now, and has welcomed you into his holy people. As Christ was anointed Priest, Prophet, and King, so may you live always as members of his body, sharing everlasting life.** *All.* **Amen.**

Clothing with White Garment

63. *Celebrant.* **(N., N.,)** (or **my dear children**) **you have become a new creation, and have clothed yourselves in Christ.
See in this white garment the outward sign of your Christian dignity.
With your family and friends to help you by word and example, bring that dignity unstained into the everlasting life of heaven.** *All.* **Amen.**

The white garments are put on the children. A different colour is not permitted unless demanded by local custom. It is desirable that the families provide the garments.

Lighted Candle

64. The celebrant takes the Easter candle and says:

Receive the light of Christ.

Someone from each family (e.g., the father or godfather) lights the child's candle from the Easter candle. If there is a large number of children, a baptismal song may be sung during the lighting of candles (see nos. 225–245, pp. 49–50 below).

Celebrant. **Parents and godparents, this light is entrusted to you to be kept burning brightly. These children of yours have been enlightened by Christ. They are to walk always as children of the light. May they keep the flame of faith alive in their hearts. When the Lord comes, may they go out to meet him with all the saints in the heavenly kingdom.**

Ephphetha or Prayer over Ears and Mouth

65. If the conference of bishops decides to preserve the practice, the rite of **Ephphetha** follows. The celebrant touches the ears and mouth of each child with his thumb, saying:

Celebrant. **The Lord Jesus made the deaf hear and the dumb speak. May he soon touch your ears to receive his word, and your mouth to proclaim his faith, to the praise and glory of God the Father.** *All.* **Amen.**

66. If the number of children is large, the celebrant says the formula once, but does not touch the ears and mouth.

Conclusion of the Rite

67. Next there is a procession to the altar, unless the baptism was performed in the sanctuary. The lighted candles are carried for the children.

A baptismal song is appropriate at this time, e.g.:

**You have put on Christ,
in him you have been baptized.
Alleluia, alleluia.**
Other songs may be chosen from nos. 225–245, pp. 49–50.

Lord's Prayer

68. The celebrant stands in front of the altar and addresses the parents, godparents, and the whole assembly in these or similar words:

Celebrant. **Dearly beloved, these children have been reborn in baptism. They are now called children of God, for so indeed they are. In confirmation they will receive the fullness of God's Spirit. In holy communion they will share the banquet of Christ's sacrifice, calling God their Father in the midst of the Church. In their name, in the Spirit of our common sonship, let us pray together in the words our Lord has given us:**

69. All present join the celebrant in singing or saying:

All. **Our Father, who art in heaven,
hallowed be thy name.
Thy kingdom come,
thy will be done
on earth as it is in heaven.
Give us this day our daily bread,
and forgive us our trespasses,
as we forgive those who trespass against us.
And lead us not into temptation,
but deliver us from evil.**

Alternative text of the Our Father, for use where permitted:

All. **Our Father in heaven,
holy be your Name,
your kingdom come,
your will be done,
on earth as in heaven.
Give us today our daily bread.
Forgive us our sins
as we forgive those who sin against us.
Do not bring us to the test
but deliver us from evil.**

Blessing

70. The celebrant first blesses the mothers, who hold the children in their arms, then the fathers, and lastly the entire assembly:

Celebrant. God the Father, through his Son, the Virgin Mary's child, has brought joy to all Christian mothers, as they see the hope of eternal life shine on their children. May he bless the mothers of these children. They now thank God for the gift of their children. May they be one with them in thanking him for ever in heaven, in Christ Jesus our Lord. *All.* Amen.

Celebrant. God is the giver of all life, human and divine. May he bless the fathers of these children. With their wives they will be the first teachers of their children in the ways of faith. May they be also the best of teachers, bearing witness to the faith by what they say and do, in Christ Jesus our Lord. *All.* Amen.

Celebrant. By God's gift, through water and the Holy Spirit, we are reborn to everlasting life. In his goodness, may he continue to pour out his blessings upon all present, who are his sons and daughters. May he make them always, wherever they may be, faithful members of his holy people. May he send his peace upon all who are gathered here, in Christ Jesus our Lord. *All.* Amen.

Celebrant. May almighty God, the Father, and the Son, ✠ and the Holy Spirit, bless you. *All.* Amen.

Other forms of the final blessing:

1. *Celebrant.* May God the almighty, who filled the world with joy by giving [247] us his only Son, bless these newly-baptized children. May they grow to be more fully like Jesus Christ our Lord. *All.* Amen.

Celebrant. May almighty God, who gives life on earth and in heaven, bless the parents of these children. They thank him now for the gift he has given them. May they always show that gratitude in action by loving and caring for their children. *All.* Amen.

Celebrant. May almighty God, who has given us a new birth by water and the Holy Spirit, generously bless all of us who are his faithful children. May we always live as his people, and may he bless all here present with his peace. *All.* Amen.

May almighty God, the Father, and the Son, ✠ and the Holy Spirit, bless you. *All.* Amen.

2. *Celebrant.* May God, the source of life and love, who fills the hearts of [248] mothers with love for their children, bless the mothers of these newly-baptized children. As they thank God for a safe delivery, may they find joy in the love, growth, and holiness of their children. *All.* Amen.

Celebrant. May God, the Father and model of all fathers, help these fathers to give good example, so that their children will grow to be mature Christians in all the fullness of Jesus Christ. *All.* Amen.

Celebrant. May God, who loves all people, bless all the relatives and friends who are gathered here. In his mercy, may he guard them from evil and give them his abundant peace. *All.* Amen.

Celebrant. And may almighty God, the Father, and the Son, ✠ and the Holy Spirit, bless you. *All.* Amen.

3. *Celebrant.* **My brothers and sisters, we entrust you all to the mercy and help** [249] **of God the almighty Father, his only Son, and the Holy Spirit. May he watch over your life, and may we all walk by the light of faith, and attain the good things he has promised us.**
Go in peace, and may almighty God, the Father, and the Son, ✠ **and the Holy Spirit, bless you.** *All.* **Amen.**

When no priest is present, the blessing is omitted.

71. After the blessing, all may sing a hymn which suitably expresses thanksgiving and Easter joy, or they may sing the song of the Blessed Virgin Mary, the *Magnificat*.
Where there is the practice of bringing baptized infants to the altar of the Blessed Virgin Mary, this custom is observed if appropriate.

RITE OF BAPTISM FOR ONE CHILD

Reception of the Child

72. If possible, baptism should take place on Sunday, the day on which the Church celebrates the paschal mystery. It should be conferred in a communal celebration in the presence of the faithful, or at least of relatives, friends, and neighbours, who are all to take an active part in the rite.

73. It is the role of the father and mother, accompanied by the godparents, to present the child to the Church for baptism.

74. The people may sing a psalm or hymn suitable for the occasion. Meanwhile the celebrating priest or deacon, vested in alb or surplice, with a stole (with or without a cope) of festive colour, and accompanied by the ministers, goes to the entrance of the church or to that part of the church where the parents and godparents are waiting with the child.

75. The celebrant greets all present, and especially the parents and godparents, reminding them briefly of the joy with which the parents welcomed this child as a gift from God, the source of life, who now wishes to bestow his own life on this little one.

76. First the celebrant questions the parents:

Celebrant. **What name do you give your child?** (or: **have you given?**)

Parents. **N.**

Celebrant. **What do you ask of God's Church for N.?**

Parents. **Baptism.**

The celebrant may choose other words for this dialogue.

The first reply may be given by someone other than the parents if local custom gives him the right to name the child. In the second response the parents may use other words, such as, 'faith,' 'the grace of Christ,' 'entrance into the Church,' 'eternal life.'

77. The celebrant speaks to the parents in these or similar words:

Celebrant. **You have asked to have your child baptized. In doing so you are accepting the responsibility of training him (her) in the practice of the faith. It will be your duty to bring him (her) up to keep God's commandments as Christ taught us, by loving God and our neighbour. Do you clearly understand what you are undertaking?**

Parents. **We do.**

78. Then the celebrant turns to the godparents and addresses them in these or similar words:

Celebrant. **Are you ready to help the parents of this child in their duty as Christian parents?**

Godparents. **We are.**

79. *Celebrant.* **N., the Christian community welcomes you with great joy. In its name I claim you for Christ our Saviour by the sign of his cross. I now trace the cross on your forehead, and invite your parents (and godparents) to do the same.**

He signs the child on the forehead, in silence. Then he invites the parents and (if it seems appropriate) the godparents to do the same.

80. The celebrant invites the parents, godparents, and the others to take part in the liturgy of the word. If circumstances permit, there is a procession to the place where this will be celebrated, during which a song is sung, e.g., Psalm 84:7, 8, 9ab.

Celebration of God's Word

Scriptural Readings and Homily

81. One or even two of the gospel passages given on pp. 19–20 above are read, during which all may sit if convenient. The passages given in the *Lectionary*, at Baptism of Infants (pp. 882–887) may be chosen, or other passages which better meet the wishes or needs of the parents. Between the readings, responsorial psalms or verses may be sung as given in the *Lectionary*.

82. After the reading, the celebrant gives a short homily, explaining to those present the significance of what has been read. His purpose will be to lead them to a deeper understanding of the mystery of baptism and to encourage the parents and godparents to a ready acceptance of the responsibilities which arise from the sacrament.

83. After the homily, or in the course of or after the litany, it is desirable to have a period of silence while all pray at the invitation of the celebrant. If convenient, a suitable song follows, such as one chosen from nos. 225–245, page 49.

Intercessions (Prayer of the Faithful)*

84. *Celebrant.* **My dear brothers and sisters, let us ask our Lord Jesus Christ to look lovingly on this child who is to be baptized, on his (her) parents and godparents, and on all the baptized.**

Leader. **By the mystery of your death and resurrection, bathe this child in light, give him (her) the new life of baptism and welcome him (her) into your holy Church.**

All. **Lord, hear our prayer.**

Leader. **Through baptism and confirmation, make him (her) your faithful follower and a witness to your gospel.**

All. **Lord, hear our prayer.**

Leader. **Lead him (her) by a holy life to the joys of God's kingdom.**

All. **Lord, hear our prayer.**

Leader. **Make the lives of his (her) parents and godparents examples of faith to inspire this child.**

All. **Lord, hear our prayer.**

Leader. **Keep his (her) family always in your love.**

All. **Lord, hear our prayer.**

Leader. **Renew the grace of our baptism in each one of us.**

All. **Lord, hear our prayer.**

Other forms may be chosen from nos. 217–220, see below pp. 46–48.

85. The celebrant next invites all present to invoke the saints.

Holy Mary, Mother of God	**pray for us**
Saint Joseph	**pray for us**
Saint John the Baptist	**pray for us**
Saint Peter and Saint Paul	**pray for us**

The names of other saints may be added, especially the patrons of the child to be baptized, and of the church or locality. The litany concludes:

All you saints of God	**pray for us**

* For England, Wales and Scotland, see footnote on p. 20.

Prayer of Exorcism and Anointing before Baptism

86. *Celebrant.* Almighty and ever-living God,
you sent your only Son into the world
to cast out the power of Satan, spirit of evil,
to rescue man from the kingdom of darkness,
and bring him into the splendour of your kingdom of light.
We pray for this child:
set him (her) free from original sin,
make him (her) a temple of your glory,
and send your Holy Spirit to dwell with him (her).
(We ask this) through Christ our Lord.   *All.* Amen.

For another form of the prayer of exorcism, see above, page 22, no. 221.

87. *Celebrant.* We anoint you with the oil of salvation
in the name of Christ our Saviour;
may he strengthen you
with his power,
who lives and reigns for ever and ever.   *All.* Amen.

He anoints the child on the breast with the oil of catechumens.

88. If, for serious reasons, the conference of bishops so decides, the anointing before baptism may be omitted. In that case the celebrant says:

Celebrant. May you have strength in the power of Christ our Saviour, who lives and reigns for ever and ever.   *All.* Amen.

And immediately he lays his hand on the child in silence.

89. Then they go to the baptistry, or to the sanctuary when baptism is celebrated there on occasion.

Celebration of the Sacrament

90. When they come to the font, the celebrant briefly reminds the congregation of the wonderful work of God whose plan it is to sanctify man, body and soul, through water. He may use these or similar words:

Celebrant. My dear brothers and sisters, we now ask God to give this child new life in abundance through water and the Holy Spirit.

or:

Celebrant. My dear brothers and sisters, God uses the sacrament of water to give his divine life to those who believe in him. Let us turn to him, and ask him to pour his gift of life from this font on this child he has chosen.

Blessing and Invocation of God over Baptismal Water (outside Easter Season)

91. Then, turning to the font, he says the following blessing:

Celebrant. Father, you give us grace through sacramental signs, which tell us of the wonders of your unseen power.
In baptism we use your gift of water, which you have made a rich symbol of the grace you give us in this sacrament.

At the very dawn of creation your Spirit breathed on the waters, making them the wellspring of all holiness.
The waters of the great flood you made a sign of the waters of baptism,
that make an end of sin and a new beginning of goodness.
Through the waters of the Red Sea you led Israel out of slavery, to be an image of God's holy people, set free from sin by baptism.
In the waters of the Jordan your Son was baptized by John and anointed with the Spirit.
Your Son willed that water and blood should flow from his side as he hung upon the cross.
After his resurrection he told his disciples: 'Go out and teach all nations, baptizing them in the name of the Father, and of the Son, and of the Holy Spirit.'
Father, look now with love upon your Church, and unseal for her the fountain of baptism.
By the power of the Spirit give to the water of this font the grace of your Son.
You created man in your own likeness: cleanse him from sin in a new birth to innocence by water and the Spirit.

The celebrant touches the water with his right hand and continues:

We ask you, Father, with your Son to send the Holy Spirit upon the water of this font. May all who are buried with Christ in the death of baptism rise also with him to newness of life. (We ask this) through Christ our Lord.   *All.* **Amen.**

Other forms may be chosen from nos. 223–224, see above pp. 23–25.

---

92. During the Easter season, if there is baptismal water which was consecrated at the Easter Vigil, the blessing and invocation of God over the water are nevertheless included, so that this theme of thanksgiving and petition may find a place in the baptism. The forms of this blessing and invocation are those given above, pp. 23–25 [nos. 223, 224], with the variation indicated at the end of each text.

Renunciation of Sin and Profession of Faith

93. The celebrant speaks to the parents and godparents in these words:

Celebrant. **Dear parents and godparents: You have come to present this child for baptism. By water and the Holy Spirit he (she) is to receive the gift of new life from God, who is love.**
On your part, you must make it your constant care to bring him (her) up in the practice of the faith. See that the divine life which God gives him (her) is kept safe from the poison of sin, to grow always stronger in his (her) heart. If your faith makes you ready to accept this responsibility, renew now the vows of your own baptism. Reject sin; profess your faith in Christ Jesus. This is the faith of the Church. This is the faith in which this child is about to be baptized.

94. The celebrant questions the parents and godparents.

Celebrant. **Do you reject Satan?**

Parents and godparents. **I do.**

Celebrant. **And all his works?**

Parents and godparents. **I do.**

Celebrant. **And all his empty promises?**

Parents and godparents. **I do.**

Celebrant. Do you reject sin, so as to live in the freedom of God's children?

Parents and godparents. I do.

Celebrant. Do you reject the glamour of evil, and refuse to be mastered by sin?

Parents and godparents. I do.

Celebrant. Do you reject Satan, father of sin and prince of darkness?

Parents and godparents. I do.

According to circumstances, this second form may be expressed with greater precision by the conferences of bishops, especially in places where it is necessary for the parents and godparents to reject superstitious and magical practices used with children.

95. Next the celebrant asks for the threefold profession of faith from the parents and godparents:

Celebrant. Do you believe in God, the Father almighty, creator of heaven and earth?

Parents and godparents. I do.

Celebrant. Do you believe in Jesus Christ, his only Son, our Lord, who was born of the Virgin Mary, was crucified, died, and was buried, rose from the dead, and is now seated at the right hand of the Father?

Parents and godparents. I do.

Celebrant. Do you believe in the Holy Spirit, the holy catholic Church, the communion of saints, the forgiveness of sins, the resurrection of the body, and life everlasting?

Parents and godparents. I do.

96. The celebrant and the congregation give their assent to this profession of faith:

Celebrant. This is our faith. This is the faith of the Church. We are proud to profess it, in Christ Jesus our Lord.   *All.* Amen.

If desired, some other formula may be used instead, or a suitable song by which the community expresses its faith with a single voice.

Baptism

97. The celebrant invites the family to the font and questions the parents and godparents:

Celebrant. Is it your will that N. should be baptized in the faith of the Church which we have all professed with you?

Parents and godparents. It is.

He baptizes the child, saying:

Celebrant. N., I baptize you in the name of the Father,

He immerses the child or pours water upon it.

and of the Son,

He immerses the child or pours water upon it a second time.

and of the Holy Spirit.

He immerses the child or pours water upon it a third time.

After the child is baptized, it is appropriate for the people to sing a short acclamation. (See nos. 225–245, pp. 49-50.)

If the baptism is performed by the pouring of water, it is preferable that the child be held by the mother (or father). Where, however, it is felt that the existing custom should be retained, the godmother (or godfather) may hold the child. If baptism is by immersion, the mother or father (godmother or godfather) lifts the child out of the font.

Anointing with Chrism

98. *Celebrant.* **God the Father of our Lord Jesus Christ has freed you from sin, given you a new birth by water and the Holy Spirit, and welcomed you into his holy people. He now anoints you with the chrism of salvation. As Christ was anointed Priest, Prophet, and King, so may you live always as a member of his body, sharing everlasting life.** *All.* **Amen.**

Then the celebrant anoints the child on the crown of the head with the sacred chrism, in silence.

Clothing with the White Garment

99. *Celebrant.* **N., you have become a new creation, and have clothed yourself in Christ. See in this white garment the outward sign of your Christian dignity. With your family and friends to help you by word and example, bring that dignity unstained into the everlasting life of heaven.** *All.* **Amen.**

The white garment is put on the child. A different colour is not permitted unless demanded by local custom. It is desirable that the family provide the garment.

Lighted Candle

100. The celebrant takes the Easter candle and says:

Celebrant. **Receive the light of Christ.**

Someone from the family (such as the father or godfather) lights the child's candle from the Easter candle.

Celebrant. **Parents and godparents, this light is entrusted to you to be kept burning brightly. This child of yours has been enlightened by Christ. He (she) is to walk always as a child of the light. May he (she) keep the flame of faith alive in his (her) heart. When the Lord comes, may he (she) go out to meet him with all the saints in the heavenly kingdom.**

Ephphetha or Prayer over Ears and Mouth

101. If the conference of bishops decides to preserve the practice, the rite of *Ephphetha* follows. The celebrant touches the ears and mouth of the child with his thumb, saying:

Celebrant. **The Lord Jesus made the deaf hear and the dumb speak. May he soon touch your ears to receive his word, and your mouth to proclaim his faith, to the praise and glory of God the Father.** *All.* **Amen.**

Conclusion of the Rite

102. Next there is a procession to the altar, unless the baptism was performed in the sanctuary. The lighted candle is carried for the child.

A baptismal song is appropriate at this time, e.g.:

**You have put on Christ,
in him you have been baptized.
Alleluia, alleluia.**

Other songs may be chosen from nos. 225–245, pp. 49-50.

Lord's Prayer

103. The celebrant stands in front of the altar and addresses the parents, godparents, and the whole assembly in these or similar words:

Celebrant. **Dearly beloved, this child has been reborn in baptism. He (she) is now called the child of God, for so indeed he (she) is. In confirmation he (she) will receive the fullness of God's Spirit. In holy communion he (she) will share the banquet of Christ's sacrifice, calling God his (her) Father in the midst of the Church. In the name of this child, in the Spirit of our common sonship, let us pray together in the words our Lord has given us:**

104. All present join the celebrant in singing or saying:

All. **Our Father, who art in heaven,**
hallowed be thy name.
Thy kingdom come.
Thy will be done on earth, as it is in heaven.
Give us this day our daily bread,
and forgive us our trespasses,
as we forgive those who trespass against us,
and lead us not into temptation,
but deliver us from evil.

Alternative text of the Our Father, for use where permitted.

All. **Our Father in heaven,**
holy be your Name,
your kingdom come,
your will be done,
on earth as in heaven.
Give us today our daily bread.
Forgive us our sins
as we forgive those who sin against us.
Do not bring us to the test
but deliver us from evil.
For the kingdom, the power, and the glory are yours,
now and for ever.

Blessing

105. The celebrant first blesses the mother, who holds the child in her arms, then the father, and lastly the entire assembly:

Celebrant. **God the Father, through his Son, the Virgin Mary's child, has brought joy to all Christian mothers, as they see the hope of eternal life shine on their children. May he bless the mother of this child. She now thanks God for the gift of her child. May she be one with him (her) in thanking him for ever in heaven, in Christ Jesus our Lord.** *All.* **Amen.**

Celebrant. **God is the giver of all life, human and divine. May he bless the father of this child. He and his wife will be the first teachers of their child in the ways of faith. May they be also the best of teachers, bearing witness to the faith by what they say and do, in Christ Jesus our Lord.** *All.* **Amen.**

Celebrant. **By God's gift, through water and the Holy Spirit, we are reborn to everlasting life. In his goodness, may he continue to pour out his blessings** upon these sons and daughters of his. May he make them always, wherever they may be, faithful members of his holy people. May he send his peace upon all who are gathered here, in Christ Jesus our Lord.   *All.* Amen.

For other forms of the blessing, see above pp. 29–30, nos. 247–249.

106. After the blessing, all may sing a hymn which suitably expresses thanksgiving and Easter joy, or they may sing the song of the Blessed Virgin Mary, the *Magnificat.*

Where there is the practice of bringing the baptized child to the altar of the Blessed Virgin Mary, this custom is observed if appropriate.

May almighty God .... (as on p. 29)

Rite of Baptism for Children in Danger of Death when no Priest or Deacon is available

157. Water, even though not blessed, is prepared for the rite. The parents, godparents, and if possible, some friends and neighbours of the family gather around the sick child. The minister, who is any suitable member of the Church, begins with this brief prayer of the faithful:

Minister. Let us ask almighty God to look with mercy on this child who is about to receive the grace of baptism, on his (her) parents and godparents, and on all baptized persons.
Through baptism, welcome this child into your Church.*

All. Lord, hear our prayer.

Minister. Through baptism, make him (her) one of your adopted children.

All. Lord, hear our prayer.

Minister. Through baptism, he (she) is being buried in the likeness of Christ's death. May he (she) also share in the glory of his resurrection.

All. Lord, hear our prayer.

Minister. Renew the grace of our baptism in each one of us.

All. Lord, hear our prayer.

Minister. May all the followers of Christ, baptized into one body, always live united in faith and love.

All. Lord, hear our prayer.

158. The prayer of the faithful concludes with this prayer:

Minister. Father of our Lord Jesus Christ,
source of all life and love,
you know the anxiety of parents
and you lighten their burden
by your fatherly care for all children in danger.
You reveal the depth of your love
by offering them a new and eternal birth.

In your kindness, hear our prayers:
keep this child from the power of sin,
and welcome him (her) with love into the kingdom of your Son.

By water and by the power of the Holy Spirit,
may this child, whom we now call N.,
share in the mystery of Christ's death
so that he (she) may also share in the mystery of Christ's resurrection.

May he (she) become your adopted son (daughter),
and share the inheritance of Christ.
Grant that he (she) may rejoice in the fellowship of your Church
with your only Son and the Holy Spirit
for ever and ever. *All.* Amen.

---

* For England, Wales and Scotland, see footnote on p. 20.

159. Then they make the profession of faith. The minister says to all present:

Minister. Let us remember our own baptism, and profess our faith in Jesus Christ. This is the faith of the Church, the faith into which children are baptized. Do you believe in God, the Father almighty, creator of heaven and earth?

All. I do.

Minister. Do you believe in Jesus Christ, his only Son, our Lord, who was born of the Virgin Mary, was crucified, died, and was buried, rose from the dead, and is now seated at the right hand of the Father?

All. I do.

Minister. Do you believe in the Holy Spirit, the holy catholic Church, the communion of saints, the forgiveness of sins, the resurrection of the body, and life everlasting?

All. I do.

The profession of faith may also be made, if desirable, by reciting the Apostles' Creed:

All. I believe in God the Father almighty,
    Creator of heaven and earth,
    and in Jesus Christ,
    his only Son, our Lord,
    who was conceived
    by the Holy Ghost,
    born of the virgin Mary,
    suffered under Pontius Pilate,
    was crucified, died and was buried;
    He descended into hell,
    the third day he arose again from the dead;
    He ascended into heaven,
    and sitteth at the right hand of God,
    the Father almighty;
    from thence he shall come
    to judge both the living and the dead.

    I believe in the Holy Ghost,
    the Holy Catholic Church,
    the communion of saints,
    the forgiveness of sins,
    the resurrection of the body,
    and life everlasting. Amen.

Alternative text of the Apostles' Creed, for use where permitted:

I believe in God, the Father almighty,
    creator of heaven and earth.

I believe in Jesus Christ, his only Son, our Lord.
    He was conceived by the power of the Holy Spirit
      and born of the Virgin Mary.
      He suffered under Pontius Pilate,
      was crucified, died and was buried.

He descended to the dead.
On the third day he rose again.
He ascended into heaven,
    and is seated at the right hand of the Father.
He will come again to judge the living and the dead.

I believe in the Holy Spirit,
    the holy catholic Church,
    the communion of saints,
    the forgiveness of sins,
    the resurrection of the body,
    and the life everlasting. Amen.

---

160. Then the minister baptizes the child, saying:

Minister: N., **I baptize you in the name of the Father,**

He pours water upon the child.

and of the Son,

He pours water upon the child a second time.

and of the Holy Spirit.

He pours water upon the child a third time.

161. Omitting all other ceremonies, he may give the white garment to the child. The minister says:

Minister. N., **you have become a new creation, and have clothed yourself in Christ.
See in this white garment the outward sign of your Christian dignity.
May you bring it unstained into the everlasting life of heaven.**

162. The minister concludes with the recitation of the Lord's Prayer:

**Our Father, who art in heaven,
hallowed be thy name.
Thy kingdom come.
Thy will be done on earth, as it is in heaven.
Give us this day our daily bread,
and forgive us our trespasses,
as we forgive those who trespass against us,
and lead us not into temptation,
but deliver us from evil.**

Alternative text of Our Father, see above, p. 37.

163. If no one there is capable of directing the prayer, any member of the Church may baptize, after reciting the Apostles' Creed, by pouring water on the child while reciting the customary words (see no. 160, above). The creed may be omitted if necessary.

164. At the moment of death, it is sufficient for the minister to omit all other ceremonies and pour water on the child while saying the usual words (see no. 160, above). It is desirable that the minister, as far as possible, should use one or two witnesses.

RITE OF BRINGING A BAPTIZED CHILD TO THE CHURCH

Reception of the Child

165. The people may sing a psalm or song suitable for the occasion. Meanwhile the celebrating priest or deacon, vested in alb or surplice, with a stole (with or without a cope) of festive colour, and accompanied by the ministers, goes to the entrance of the church where the parents and godparents are waiting with the child.

166. The celebrant greets all present, and especially the parents and godparents. He praises them for having had the child baptized without delay, and thanks God and congratulates the parents on the child's return to health.

167. First the celebrant questions the parents:

Celebrant. **What name have you given your child?**

Parents. N.

Celebrant. **What do you ask of God's Church, now that your child has been baptized?**

Parents. **We ask that the whole community will know that he (she) has been received into the Church.**

The first reply may be given by someone other than the parents if local custom gives him the right to name the child. In the second response the parents may use other words, such as 'that he (she) is a Christian,' 'that he (she) has been baptized.'

168. Then the celebrant speaks to the parents in these or similar words:

Celebrant. **Do you realize that in bringing your child to the Church, you are accepting the duty of raising him (her) in the faith, so that by observing the commandments he (she) will love God and neighbour as Christ taught us?**

Parents: **We do.**

169. Then the celebrant turns to the godparents and addresses them in these or similar words:

Celebrant. **Are you ready to help the mother and father of this child to carry out their duty as Christian parents?**

Godparents. **We are.**

170. *Celebrant.* **N., the Christian community welcomes you with great joy, now that you have recovered your health. We now bear witness that you have been received as a member of the Church. In the name of the community I sign you with the cross of Christ, who gave you a new life in baptism and made you a member of his Church. I invite your parents (and godparents) to do the same.**

He signs the child on the forehead, in silence. Then he invites the parents and (if it seems appropriate) the godparents to do the same.

171. The celebrant invites the parents, godparents, and all who are present to take part in the liturgy of the word. If circumstances permit, there is a procession to the place where this will be celebrated, during which a song is sung, such as Psalm 84:7, 8, 9ab.

Celebration of God's Word

Scriptural Readings and Homily

172. One or even two of the gospel passages given above, pp. 19–20, no. 44, are read, during which all may sit if convenient. Other passages from the *Lectionary* may be read instead, or passages which better meet the needs or wishes of the parents (such as 1 Kings 17:17–24; 2 Kings 4:8–37).

Between the readings, responsorial psalms or verses may be sung, as given in the *Lectionary* (at Baptism of Infants, pp. 882–887).

173. After the reading, the celebrant gives a brief homily, explaining to those present the significance of what has been read. His purpose will be to lead them to a deeper understanding of the mystery of baptism and to encourage parents and godparents to a ready acceptance of the responsibilities which arise from the sacrament.

174. After the homily, or in the course of or after the litany, it is desirable to have a period of silence while all pray at the invitation of the celebrant. A suitable hymn may follow, such as one chosen from nos. 225–245.

Prayer of the Faithful ∗

175. *Celebrant.* Let us ask our Lord Jesus Christ to look lovingly on this child, on his (her) parents and godparents, and on all the baptized.

Leader. May this child always show gratitude to God for his (her) baptism and recovery.

All. Lord, hear our prayer.

Leader. Help him (her) always to be a living member of your Church.

All. Lord, hear our prayer.

Leader. Inspire him (her) to hear, follow, and witness to your gospel.

All. Lord, hear our prayer.

Leader. May he (she) come with joy to the table of your sacrifice.

All. Lord, hear our prayer.

Leader. Help him (her) to love God and neighbour as you have taught us.

All. Lord, hear our prayer.

Leader. May he (she) grow in holiness and wisdom by listening to his (her) fellow Christians and following their example.

All. Lord, hear our prayer.

Leader. Keep all your followers united in faith and love for ever.

All. Lord, hear our prayer.

176. The celebrant next invites all present to invoke the saints:

Holy Mary, Mother of God	pray for us
Saint Joseph	pray for us
Saint John the Baptist	pray for us
Saint Peter and Saint Paul	pray for us

The names of other saints may be added, especially the patrons of the child and of the church or locality.

The litany concludes:

All you saints of God	pray for us

177. *Celebrant.* Father of our Lord Jesus Christ,
source of all life and love,
you are glorified by the loving care
these parents have shown this child.
You rescue children from danger and save them in baptism.

∗ For England, Wales and Scotland, see footnote on p. 20.

Your Church thanks you and prays for your child N.
You have brought him (her) out of the kingdom of darkness
and into your marvellous light.
You have made him (her) your adopted child
and a temple of the Holy Spirit.

Help him (her) in all the dangers of this life
and strengthen him (her) in the constant effort to reach your
   kingdom,
through the power of Christ our Saviour.
(We ask this) through Christ our Lord.   *All.* **Amen.**

Further Rites

Anointing with Chrism

178. *Celebrant.* **God the Father of our Lord Jesus Christ has freed you from sin, given you a new birth by water and the Holy Spirit, and welcomed you into his holy people. He now anoints you with the chrism of salvation. As Christ was anointed Priest, Prophet, and King, so may you live always as a member of his body, sharing everlasting life.**   *All.* **Amen.**

Then the celebrant anoints the child on the crown of the head with the chrism, in silence.

Clothing with White Garment

179. *Celebrant.* **N., you have become a new creation, and have clothed yourself in Christ. See in this white garment the outward sign of your Christian dignity. With your family and friends to help you by word and example, bring that dignity unstained into the everlasting life of heaven.**   *All.* **Amen.**

Lighted Candle

180. The celebrant takes the Easter candle and says:

Celebrant. **Receive the Light of Christ.**

Someone, such as the father or godfather, lights the child's candle from the Easter candle. The celebrant then says:

Celebrant. **Parents and godparents, this light is entrusted to you to be kept burning brightly. This child of yours has been enlightened by Christ. He (she) is to walk always as a child of the light. May he (she) keep the flame of faith alive in his (her) heart. When the Lord comes, may he (she) go out to meet him with all the saints in the heavenly kingdom.**

A baptismal song is appropriate at this time, such as:

**You have put on Christ,
in him you have been baptized.
Alleluia, alleluia.**

Other songs may be chosen from nos. 225–245, pp. 49–50.

Conclusion of the Rite

Lord's Prayer

181. The celebrant stands in front of the altar and addresses the parents, godparents, and the whole assembly in these or similar words:

Celebrant. **My dear brothers and sisters, this child has been reborn in baptism. He (she) is now called the child of God, for so indeed he (she) is. In confirmation** he (she) will receive the fullness of God's Spirit. In holy communion he (she) will share the banquet of Christ's sacrifice, calling God his (her) Father in the midst of the Church. In the name of this child, in the spirit of our common sonship, let us pray together in the words our Lord has given us:

182. All present join the celebrant in singing or saying:

All. Our Father, who art in heaven,
Hallowed be thy name.
Thy kingdom come.
Thy will be done on earth, as it is in heaven.
Give us this day our daily bread,
And forgive us our trespasses,
As we forgive those who trespass against us,
And lead us not into temptation,
But deliver us from evil.

Alternative text of Our Father, see above, p. 37.

Blessing

183. The celebrant first blesses the mother, who holds the child in her arms, then the father, and lastly the entire assembly:

Celebrant. God the Father, through his Son, the Virgin Mary's child, has brought joy to all Christian mothers, as they see the hope of eternal life shine on their children. May he bless the mother of this child. She now thanks God for the gift of her child. May she be one with her son (daughter) in thanking God for ever in heaven, in Christ Jesus our Lord.   *All.* Amen.

Celebrant. God is the giver of all life, human and divine. May he bless the father of this child. He and his wife will be the first teachers of their child in the ways of faith. May they also be the best of teachers, bearing witness to the faith by what they say and do, in Christ Jesus our Lord.   *All.* Amen.

Celebrant. By God's gift, through water and the Holy Spirit, we are reborn to ever-lasting life. In his goodness, may he continue to pour out his blessings on these sons and daughters of his. May he make them always, wherever they may be, faithful members of his holy people. May he send his peace upon all who are gathered here, in Christ Jesus our Lord.   *All.* Amen.

Celebrant. May almighty God, the Father, and the Son, ✠ and the Holy Spirit, bless you.   *All.* Amen.

For other forms of the blessing, see above, pp. 29–30, nos. 247–249.

184. After the blessing, all may sing a hymn which suitably expresses thanksgiving and Easter joy, or they may sing the song of the Blessed Virgin Mary, the *Magnificat*.

Where there is the practice of bringing the baptized child to the altar of the Blessed Virgin, this custom is observed if appropriate.

185. The above rite is followed even when the baptized child is brought to the church after other difficulties (such as persecution, disagreement between parents) which prevented the celebration of baptism in the church. In such cases, the celebrant should adapt the explanations, readings, intentions in the prayer of the faithful and other parts of the rite to the child's circumstances.

OTHER FORMS OF THE PRAYER OF THE FAITHFUL

Any one of the following forms given in this baptismal ritual may be used for the prayer of the faithful. Petitions may be added or omitted at will, taking into consideration the special circumstances of each family. The prayer always concludes with the invocation of the saints.*

1.

216. As given above in no. 47, p. 20 above.

2.

217. We have been called by the Lord to be a royal priesthood, a holy nation, a people he has acquired for himself. Let us ask him to show his mercy to these children, who are to receive the graces of baptism, to their parents and godparents, and to all the baptized everywhere.

Through baptism, bring these children into your Church.

R. Lord, hear our prayer.

Throughout their lives, help them to be faithful witnesses to your Son, Jesus Christ, for they are being marked with his cross.

R. Lord, hear our prayer.

As they are being buried in the likeness of Christ's death through baptism, may they also share in the glory of Christ's resurrection.

R. Lord, hear our prayer.

Teach them by the words and example of their parents and godparents, and help them to grow strong as living members of the Church.

R. Lord, hear our prayer.

Renew the grace of baptism in each of us here.

R. Lord, hear our prayer.

May all Christ's followers, baptized into one body, always live united in faith and love.

R. Lord, hear our prayer.

The invocation of the saints follows.

3.

218. My fellow Christians, let us ask the mercy of Jesus Christ our Lord for these children who will receive the gift of baptism, for their parents and godparents, and for all baptized persons.

Through baptism, make these children God's own sons and daughters.

R. Lord, hear our prayer.

---

* For England and Wales, see footnote on p. 20.

Help these tender branches grow to be more like you, the true vine, and be your faithful followers.

R. Lord, hear our prayer.

May they always keep your commands, walk in your love, and proclaim your Good News to their fellow men.

R. Lord, hear our prayer.

May they be counted as God's friends through your saving work, Lord Jesus and may they inherit eternal life.

R. Lord, hear our prayer.

Help their parents and godparents to lead them to know and love God.

R. Lord, hear our prayer.

Inspire all men to share in the new birth of baptism.

R. Lord, hear our prayer.

The invocation of the saints follows.

4.

219. We have been called by the Lord to be a royal priesthood, a holy nation, a people he has acquired for himself. Let us ask him to show his mercy to these children, who are to receive the graces of baptism, to their parents and godparents, and to all the baptized everywhere.

Through baptism may these children become God's own beloved sons and daughters. We pray to the Lord.

R. Lord, hear our prayer.

Once they are born again of water and the Holy Spirit, may they always live in that Spirit, and make their new life known to their fellow men. We pray to the Lord.

R. Lord, hear our prayer.

Help them to triumph over the deceits of the devil and the attractions of evil. We pray to the Lord.

R. Lord, hear our prayer.

May they love you, Lord, with all their heart, soul, mind and strength, and love their neighbour as themselves. We pray to the Lord.

R. Lord, hear our prayer.

Help all of us here to be models of faith for these children. We pray to the Lord.

R. Lord, hear our prayer.

May all Christ's faithful people, who received the sign of the cross at baptism, always and everywhere give witness to him by the way they live. We pray to the Lord.

R. **Lord, hear our prayer.**

The invocation of the saints follows.

5.

220. **Let us ask Christ's mercy for these children, their parents and godparents, and all baptized Christians.**

Give them a new birth to eternal life through water and the Holy Spirit.

R. **Lord, hear our prayer.**

Help them always to be living members of your Church.

R. **Lord, hear our prayer.**

Inspire them to hear and follow your gospel, and to give witness to you by their lives. We ask this, Lord.

R. **Lord, hear our prayer.**

May they come with joy to the table of your sacrifice.

R. **Lord, hear our prayer.**

Help them to love God and neighbour as you have taught us.

R. **Lord, hear our prayer.**

May they grow in holiness and wisdom by listening to their fellow Christians and by following their example.

R. **Lord, hear our prayer.**

Let all your followers remain united in faith and love.

R. **Lord, hear our prayer.**

The invocation of the saints follows.

ACCLAMATIONS AND HYMNS

225. Lord God, who is your equal?
Strong, majestic, and holy!
Worthy of praise, worker of wonders! (Exodus 51:11)

226. God is light: in him there is no darkness. (1 John 1:5)

227. God is love: he who lives in love, lives in God. (1 John 4:16)

228. There is one God, one Father of all:
he is over all, and through all:
he lives in all of us. (Ephesians 4:6)

229. Come to him and receive his light! (Psalm 33:6)

230. Blessed be God who chose you in Christ. (see Ephesians 1:4)

231. You are God's work of art, created in Christ
Jesus. (Ephesians 2:10)

232. You are now God's children, my
dearest friends.
What you shall be in his glory has not
yet been revealed. (1 John 3:2)

233. Think of how God loves you!
He calls you his own children,
and that is what you are. (1 John 3:1)

234. Happy are those who have washed their robes
clean:
washed in the blood of the Lamb! (Revelation 22:14)

235. All of you are one:
united in Christ Jesus. (Galatians 3:28)

236. Imitate God, walk in his love,
just as Christ loves us. (Ephesians 5:1–2)

Hymns in the Style of the New Testament

237. Praised be the Father of our Lord Jesus Christ:
a God so merciful and kind!
He has given us a new birth, a living hope,
by raising Jesus his Son from death.
Salvation is our undying inheritance,
preserved for us in heaven,
salvation at the end of time. (1 Peter 1:3–5)

238. How great the sign of God's love for us,
     Jesus Christ our Lord:
     promised before all time began,
     revealed in these last days.
     He lived and suffered and died for us,
     but the Spirit raised him to life.
     People everywhere have heard his message
     and placed their faith in him.
     What wonderful blessings he gives his people:
     living in the Father's glory,
     he fills all creation
     and guides it to perfection.

Songs from Ancient Liturgies

239. We believe in you, Lord Jesus Christ.
     Fill our hearts with your radiance,
     and make us the children of light!

240. We come to you, Lord Jesus.
     Fill us with your life,
     make us children of the Father,
     and one in you.

241. Lord Jesus, from your wounded side
     flowed streams of cleansing water:
     the world was washed of all its sin,
     all life made new again!

242. The Father's voice calls us above the waters,
     the glory of the Son shines on us,
     the love of the Spirit fills us with life.

243. Holy Church of God, stretch out your hand
     and welcome your children
     newborn of water
     and of the Spirit of God.

244. Rejoice, you newly baptized,
     chosen members of the kingdom.
     Buried with Christ in death,
     you are reborn in him by faith.

245. This is the fountain of life,
     water made holy by the suffering of Christ,
     washing all the world.
     You who are washed in this water
     have hope of heaven's kingdom.

BLESSING AND INVOCATION OF GOD OVER BAPTISMAL WATER

To be used when no priest is present

141. With the parents and godparents carrying the children who are to be baptized, the catechist comes to the font. He invites all to pray:

Catechist. My dear brothers and sisters, let us ask God to give these children new life in abundance through water and the Holy Spirit.

142. If there is no blessed water available, the catechist stands before the font and says this invocation:

Merciful Father, from the font of baptism you have given us new life as your sons and daughters.

All. Blessed be God *(or some other suitable acclamation by the people).*

Catechist. You bring together all who are baptized in water and the Holy Spirit to be one people in Jesus Christ your Son.

All. Blessed be God.

Catechist. You have made us free by pouring the Spirit of your love into our hearts, so that we will enjoy your peace.

All. Blessed be God.

Catechist. You have chosen your baptized people to announce with joy the Good News of Christ to all nations.

All. Blessed be God.

Catechist. Come and bless this water in which your servants are to be baptized. You have called them to the washing of new life in the faith of your Church, so that they may have eternal life. (We ask this) through Christ our Lord.

All. Amen.

143. If blessed water is available, he says the following invocation:

Father of our Lord Jesus Christ,
source of all life and love,
you are glorified throughout the world
by the simple joys and daily cares
of mothers and fathers.

In the beauty of a child's birth
and in the mystery of his rebirth to eternal life,
you give us a glimpse of all creation:
it is guided by your fatherly love,
unfolding in fruitfulness to perfection
in Jesus Christ your Son.

In your kindness
hear the prayers of the Church and of these parents.
Look upon these children with love,
and keep them from the power of sin.
Since they are a gift from you, Father,
welcome them into the kingdom of your Son.

You have created this water,
and made it clean, refreshing, and life-giving.
You have made it holy through the baptism of Christ,
that by the power of the Holy Spirit
it may give your people a new birth.

When these children are baptized into the mystery
of Christ's suffering, death, and resurrection,
may they be worthy to become members of your Church,
your very own children.
Father, may they rejoice
with Jesus your Son and the Holy Spirit
for ever and ever.

All. **Amen.**